Great Ideas of Science

EVOLUTION

by Paul Fleisher

Twenty-First Century Books
Minneapolis

Twenty-First Century Books
A division of Lerner Publishing Group
241 First Avenue North
Minneapolis, Minnesota 55401 U.S.A.

Website address: www.lernerbooks.com

Library of Congress Cataloging-in-Publication Data

Fleisher, Paul.
    Evolution / by Paul Fleisher.
        p.   cm. — (Great ideas of science)
    Includes bibliographical references and index.
    ISBN-13: 978–0–8225–2134–1 (lib. bdg. : alk. paper)
    ISBN-10: 0–8225–2134–2 (lib. bdg. : alk. paper)
    1. Evolution (Biology)—Juvenile literature. I. Title. II. Series.
QH367.1.F59 2006
576.8—dc22   2004028897

Manufactured in the United States of America
1 2 3 4 5 6 – BP – 11 10 09 08 07 06

TABLE OF CONTENTS

The world is full of an amazing diversity of creatures. Look outside your window. You'll see animals and plants of all shapes and sizes. What's more, millions of species live in other parts of the world. There are worlds of microscopic creatures you can't see. Fantastic creatures live in the depths of the ocean, between grains of soil, beneath the leaves of the rain forest, and high in the cold, stony mountains.

Biologists estimate as many as thirty million different species live on Earth. Scientists think these modern creatures represent only about 1 percent of all species that have ever lived on our planet. The variety of life is truly astounding.

Until the 1800s, most people—including philosophers and scientists—believed a creator-god must have made each plant and animal. It seemed as if a creator were required. After all, living things are incredibly complex. Organisms sense the world around them. They capture and digest food and turn it into energy. They circulate oxygen, eliminate waste, and produce offspring. Could such complicated creatures come to be on their own?

British clergyman William Paley used the example of a pocket watch. Suppose you came upon a timepiece lying in a meadow. Examining it, you'd find interconnected gears, springs, and levers moving the hands around the face in a regular motion. Such an object could not just appear. Surely it must have been made by some unseen craftsperson. The workings of a living creature are at least as complex as a watch. That complexity, Paley said, was evidence of a creator.

On the other hand, evidence that life changes over time was growing year by year. Explorers were finding fossils of creatures that no longer lived on Earth. Their body structures were different from modern-day animals and plants. But they were similar enough to suggest that the living things in our world might have evolved from them.

The records of the evolution of horses and whales are particularly complete. Their fossils show a clear progression. Over many millions of years, a series of ancestor species gradually evolved to become present-day horses (see diagram below) and modern whales.

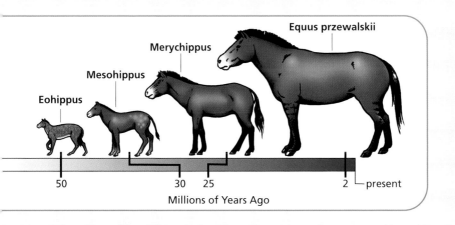

Equus przewalskii

Merychippus

Mesohippus

Eohippus

50   30   25   2 └ present
Millions of Years Ago

Life evolves. Living things change to meet different challenges over time. The evidence is overwhelming. We can see evolution happening almost before our eyes. Bacteria evolve resistance to antibiotic drugs in just a few years. Many insects—boll weevils, potato beetles, and houseflies, to name a few—have evolved resistance to pesticides.

Biologists find evidence for evolution in the similarities among organisms. For example, birds, mammals, reptiles, and amphibians all have four homologous (very similar) limbs. They all share the same basic bone structure. The limbs have evolved to become a wide variety of legs, arms, and wings. But the shared anatomy means these widely

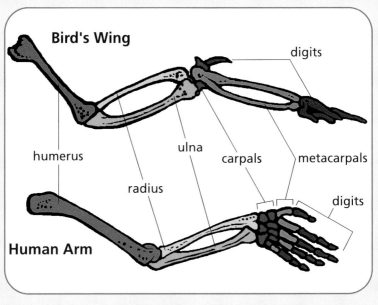

The similarity in the structure of a bird's wing and the human arm is one example scientists point to as evidence for evolution

different groups of creatures must have descended from a common four-legged ancestor.

The problem facing nineteenth-century biologists was finding the cause for evolution. In 1858 Charles Darwin found an explanation for how evolution happens. His theory has successfully withstood 150 years of careful scientific testing. It has met every challenge. For example,

This portrait of Charles Darwin was painted in 1840.

Darwin's theory predicts that there must be ancestor species that evolved into the creatures populating our world today. Scientists find more of these fossil ancestors every year.

Evolutionary puzzles still remain to be solved, both among living organisms and in the record of ancient fossils. But Darwin's theory is recognized by biologists as the best way to solve those mysteries. His idea is essential to understanding life on Earth.

CHAPTER 1

EVOLUTION: FACT AND THEORY

EVOLUTION BEFORE DARWIN

The idea that life evolves did not originate with Darwin. Even in ancient times, a few Greek philosophers thought living things could change form over time. Some early Christian scholars doubted that Noah's ark could have held all the species of Earth. They thought some creatures must have arisen after the biblical flood. But scientific study of evolution really began in eighteenth-century France.

In the late 1700s, the French naturalist Georges-Louis LeClerc de Buffon divided Earth's history into geological eras. Based on fossil evidence, he recognized that different creatures had lived in different periods. However, Buffon believed the later species arose separately, rather than evolving from earlier ones.

In the early 1800s, French scientist Georges Cuvier studied fossils of mammoths and other mammals. He showed that they were clearly different from animals alive in his time. He thought the extinct animals had been destroyed by catastrophes such as climate changes or floods such as the one described in the Bible. Cuvier, too, rejected the idea that species could change. But his studies added to the growing evidence that life on Earth has changed over time.

In 1809 another French scientist, Jean-Baptiste de Lamarck, went much further. He said species evolve from "lower" to "higher" forms. Like many others, Lamarck saw humanity as the highest product of this process. Lamarck also thought organisms adapt to their environment by using or disusing parts of their bodies. For example, he suggested that early giraffes developed long necks by stretching to reach the leaves of tall trees. Somehow, reaching enabled the giraffes to change their shape. That change was then passed on to their offspring.

Most scientists rejected Lamarck's ideas for lack of proof. He had no evidence that such changes actually take place. But the hunt was on for something that could explain how species evolve.

The scientist with the greatest influence on Darwin's thinking was probably Scottish geologist Charles Lyell. In 1830 Lyell published *Principles of Geology*. In that book, he detailed evidence that Earth changes gradually over long periods of time. And he described the geological processes responsible for that change: volcanoes spew lava, sea levels rise and fall, sediments settle to the ocean floor, and mountains are pushed up from ancient seas. Lyell showed that Earth and its creatures have existed for a very long time.

DARWIN ON THE *BEAGLE*

Charles Darwin's father, a wealthy British physician, sent his son to school to become a doctor or a clergyman. But Charles was more interested in nature study. As a young man of twenty-one, he joined the crew of the *Beagle* as the ship's naturalist. The *Beagle,* a 90-foot (30-meter) sailing ship captained by Robert Fitzroy, was about to sail on an expedition to map the coast of South America. Charles Darwin had never been to sea.

During the five-year voyage, Darwin spent much of his time ashore. His first stop en route to South America was the mountainous Cape Verde Islands, off the coast of Africa. There he saw ancient fossils that had been lifted

Charles Darwin sailed on the *Beagle* to explore South America. The animals he saw on his voyage contributed to his theories about evolution.

thousands of feet above the sea. Darwin had been reading Charles Lyell's book. He was convinced, as Lyell had been, that Earth is ancient and ever changing.

As he explored South America, Darwin took careful notes and gathered thousands of specimens to send back to England. He also collected fossils of creatures that no longer exist anywhere in the modern world.

On February 20, 1835, Chile experienced a devastating earthquake. A few days later, Darwin walked along the

THE VOYAGE OF THE *BEAGLE* AROUND SOUTH AMERICA, 1831–1836

Chilean coast where the *Beagle* was anchored. Darwin was stunned by the destruction caused by the earthquake. But he was also amazed to see geological changes happen before his eyes. The quake had lifted ledges of rock—sea creatures still attached—several feet above the waterline.

A few days later, high in Chile's Andes Mountains, Darwin saw fossilized seashells trapped in the layers of limestone. These creatures had once lived in an ancient ocean. Now they were preserved in stone, 14,000 feet (4,300 m) above sea level. The twenty-six-year-old naturalist marveled at earth-building forces powerful enough to lift the seabed up to form tall mountains. Seeing evidence of a changing Earth made a lasting impression on Darwin. He tried to imagine the vast expanses of time needed to accomplish such great changes.

Several months after the earthquake, Darwin visited his most famous destination—the Galápagos Islands. The Galápagos are a group of small volcanic islands 600 miles (970 kilometers) off the coast of Ecuador. The plants and animals Darwin saw there were unique. He found giant tortoises, swimming iguanas, and a fascinating array of finches and other birds. Later, he realized the creatures on each island were different species. Each had slightly different physical features. This was puzzling, since the islands were quite close together. He wondered why each island was populated by similar but distinctly different species.

Darwin began searching for an explanation for this great scientific mystery: How did the great diversity of life come to be? Why are there millions of different kinds of

GEOLOGICAL ERAS Geologists divide the history of Earth into time periods. The largest of these divisions are known as eras. There are four geological eras, the Precambrian, Paleozoic, Mesozoic, and Cenozoic. Each era is divided into periods. And in some cases, periods are further divided into epochs. This chart outlines the major time divisions in Earth's history:

Era	Period	Epoch	Duration	Start Time
Cenozoic (Age of Mammals)			65 million years	65 million years ago
Mesozoic (Age of Reptiles)	Cretaceous		80	145
	Jurassic		68	213
	Triassic		35	248
Paleozoic (Ancient Life-Forms)	Permian		38	286
	Carboniferous	Pennsylvanian	74	360
		Mississippian		
	Devonian		50	410
	Silurian		30	440
	Ordovician		60	500
	Cambrian		30	530
Precambrian			4 billion years	4500

plants and animals? Could all those creatures have been made by a creator in six days, or was there another explanation that could meet the tests of scientific observation?

On October 20, 1836, the *Beagle* finally returned to London. Darwin never left England again. He had gathered enough information and ideas to last a lifetime.

CHAPTER 2

DARWIN TACKLES EVOLUTION

After he returned to England, Darwin published the journal of his journey. That book, called *The Voyage of the Beagle,* was a big hit among British readers. It still makes fascinating reading today.

Darwin married his cousin Emma Wedgwood. They established a home at Down House, a small estate in the countryside near London. There in his study, Darwin considered the question of how life evolved.

He examined thousands of specimens from his trip and from other sources. He wrote many letters, exchanging ideas with biologists, geologists, and plant and animal breeders. He read and studied and thought, but the cause of evolution remained a puzzle. Then, in 1838, Darwin happened to read economist Thomas Malthus's *Essay on the Principle of Population.*

Malthus pointed out that human populations grow much faster than the resources needed to feed, clothe, and house them. (Malthus wrote long before effective

This cluttered room is the study where Darwin formed his theory of evolution.

forms of birth control were developed.) As a result, he said, people would always compete for scarce resources. People without enough resources would be unable to feed their children. Many people would die without producing children of their own.

Darwin realized that Malthus's vision would hold true for any species. Immediately, he knew he had the key to understanding evolution. He wrote: "As many more individuals are produced than can possibly survive, there must in every case be a struggle for existence, either one individual with another of the same species, or with the individuals of distinct species, or with the physical conditions of life."

Darwin's revolutionary theory is surprisingly simple. It is built on just a few basic ideas:

1. Life has existed on Earth for vast amounts of time.
2. All creatures produce more offspring than can possibly survive.

3. Offspring resemble their parents. Characteristics are passed from one generation to the next.
4. Individuals in each species vary from one another in small ways.
5. Nature selects the most successful variations. Individuals with traits that favor their survival are more likely to have offspring of their own.

Darwin realized that species evolve over thousands of generations through a process he called natural selection. Every environment has dangers and limited resources. Individual organisms with traits that help them compete successfully are more fit—more likely to survive. This process is often called survival of the fittest, a phrase first used by one of Darwin's early supporters, Herbert Spencer.

Traits are hereditary. Creatures with traits that help them survive long enough to reproduce pass those advantages to their offspring. Every creature alive today is descended from millions of generations of survivors, each of which had traits that allowed it to reproduce successfully.

Natural Selection

Darwin realized that natural selection must work much like selective breeding, or artificial selection. Gardeners save seeds from their most beautiful or unusual flowers and their best crops. A sheep farmer mates the ewes and rams that produce the best quality wool. In this way, growers improve their crops and develop new varieties.

Darwin asked farmers how they bred livestock, flowers, or vegetables for particular characteristics—size, rapid growth, or productivity, for example. He understood that nature sim-

Above: a short-legged ram *(right)* and a long-legged ewe *(left)* produce offspring with very short legs *(center).* In 1791 a farmer from Massachusetts kept breeding the sheep with the shortest legs until he had a whole flock of short-legged sheep that couldn't jump over his fences and escape.

ilarly selects the most successful traits, by allowing individuals with those traits to survive long enough to reproduce.

Darwin knew his idea would be controversial. By 1844 he had written a first draft of his great work, *The Origin of Species by Means of Natural Selection.* But he was not yet ready to publish. He wanted more evidence to support his theory. He spent more than ten years studying the life cycles of barnacles and other creatures. In 1858 Darwin was still gathering evidence. But then a letter arrived that forced him to make his work public.

MEANWHILE, IN THE SOUTH PACIFIC...

Charles Darwin wasn't the only person wondering about evolution. Far from England, another British naturalist,

Alfred Russel Wallace

Alfred Russel Wallace, was tackling the same puzzle.

Unlike Darwin, Wallace was raised in a relatively poor family. At fourteen he quit school to find work in London. But Wallace was enormously curious. With the support of an older brother, he continued to experiment, observe, and educate himself.

In 1848 Wallace began a four-year expedition to South America to study the plants and animals of the Amazon River. His trip was inspired in part by Darwin's book, *The Voyage of the Beagle.* Wallace financed his trip by selling the plant and animal specimens he gathered to European collectors.

The journey was a dangerous one. Wallace and his companions traveled through a wilderness of intense heat, stinging insects, venomous snakes, and tropical diseases. He wrote articles and collected enough specimens to make the expedition a financial success. He collected almost fifteen thousand different species, about half of which had never been seen in Europe. Wallace was most interested in the locations where different species were found. He thought new species might arise when populations of a single species are separated by geography so they can no longer breed with one another.

Unfortunately, on the return trip to England in 1852, Wallace's ship caught fire. Most of his notes and draw-

Indonesia—The Malay Archipelago

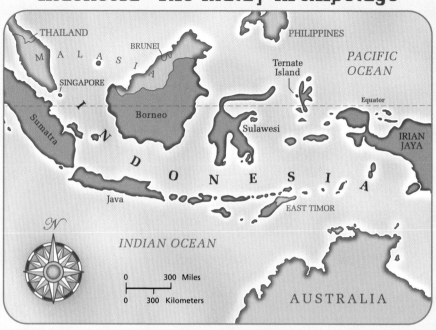

ings and many specimens were lost. He and the crew were lucky to survive.

Wallace spent about a year and a half in England. He attended scientific gatherings and even met Darwin briefly. But his travels were far from over. In 1854 he set off for the Malay Archipelago. This is a group of many islands north of Australia. This trip lasted eight years. Wallace collected many thousands of specimens. His observations led him to a theory of evolution almost identical to Darwin's.

Wallace's study of island life gave him the key to the mystery of evolution. As Darwin found on the Galápagos, islands keep populations apart. Each separate population develops differently, depending on the conditions on its island.

Eventually, each group evolves into a different species. Imagine a type of rodent that migrates to two neighboring islands, for example. Each island has different geography, different foods, different predators. Perhaps one island is rich in edible fruits, while the other is not. On the first island, the rodents evolve to take advantage of the energy-rich fruits. Meanwhile, the other group eats leaves, bark, and insects. After many generations, the teeth and digestive systems of the two populations have become so different they must be considered two separate species.

In 1858 Wallace was studying the island of Ternate. During a feverish bout of malaria, he had a moment of inspiration. Like Darwin, he, too, thought of Malthus's *Essay on the Principle of Population.* Far more creatures are born than can possibly survive. He realized that the struggle for existence was the engine that drives evolution.

Wallace quickly wrote a twelve-page paper, "On the Tendency of Varieties to Depart Indefinitely from the Original Type." Weaker animals die, he wrote, while only "the most perfect in health and vigour—those who are best able to obtain food regularly and avoid their numerous enemies" live extended lives. The same would be true of whole groups of animals. Better-adapted varieties would thrive. Others would become less common or die out.

As one variety succeeded, he wrote, it would replace the species from which it arose with "a more perfectly developed and more highly organized form." The new species could never go back to its original form. Each species would vary further and further from its original type. With enough time, this process could produce the wonderful diversity of life Wallace knew from his tropical journeys. In March 1858, Wallace finished his manuscript. He mailed it to the scientist he knew would be most interested—Charles Darwin!

The manuscript traveled by ship to England. Darwin received it on June 18, 1858. Its arrival set off a great crisis. In science the first person to discover a new idea gets the credit. Darwin had planned to work for several more years before publishing his theory. But suddenly another researcher had arrived at a similar idea. Darwin didn't want to lose credit for solving the mystery of evolution.

Darwin immediately told his friends Charles Lyell and Joseph Hooker—both respected British scientists—about Wallace's letter. They arranged a meeting at which Darwin's and Wallace's papers would both be read. Darwin's draft from fourteen years earlier would be read first. They wrote Wallace of the plan. He was satisfied. Wallace was pleased that his work would appear on the same program with that of the famous Charles Darwin, even if he did get second billing.

On July 1, 1858, at a meeting of the Linnaean Society of London, Darwin's 1844 manuscript was read, along with Wallace's paper. Neither man was present. Darwin quickly began completing his book. *The Origin of Species by Means of Natural Selection* was published the following year.

Wallace lost his chance for fame as the first man to explain evolution. But when he returned to England in 1862, he was welcomed into the company of scientists. For the rest of his life, Wallace led an amazingly productive career. He wrote hundreds of scientific papers and books and identified thousands of new species.

CHAPTER 3

DARWIN'S THEORY IN DETAIL

People sometimes dismiss Darwin's ideas as "just a theory," as if it were just one of a number of possible guesses about how life evolves. But a scientific theory is much more than just a guess. A scientific theory is a thorough, detailed explanation for a wide range of facts and observations. A theory also predicts the results of future observations and discoveries. If later discoveries agree with the predictions, the theory is supported. If not, scientists must change their theory or look for a better one.

Darwin's theory has been refined as scientists learned the details of how heredity works. But his basic explanation of natural selection as the force behind evolution has grown ever more certain. It has become the most basic principle of biology.

Darwin's theory of evolution is based on a few simple ideas. Let's look at each of them more closely.

LIFE HAS EXISTED ON EARTH FOR VAST AMOUNTS OF TIME Darwin's theory of evolution depends on an almost unimaginably long period of time. Organisms must have passed through many millions of generations to have evolved into the life we know today.

How old is Earth? In 1658 Archbishop James Ussher used the Bible to calculate the age of our planet. After careful figuring, he announced that God had created Earth on October 22, 4004 B.C.

But Ussher's estimate didn't match the evidence. Many mountains are made of layer after layer of sedimentary rock, some containing fossils of ancient sea life. In the late 1700s, geologist James Hutton described how such layers form. Sediments gradually settle out of the ocean water. These sediments accumulate *very* slowly—about 1 centimeter (about 0.4 inch) every hundred years. They slowly compress into sandstone, shale, or limestone. Later, geological forces push these layers up to form mountain ranges thousands of feet high. All this takes time. In 1830 Charles Lyell expanded on Hutton's work. He detailed more evidence that Earth has changed slowly and gradually over great periods of time.

By Darwin's time, scientists understood that Earth is very old. Just how old, however, was still a mystery. Earth began as a ball of molten rock. Researchers tried to estimate how long the planet would have taken to cool to its present temperature. Those estimates ranged into the millions of years. Estimates based on the rate that sediments accumulate gave similar numbers. Both methods greatly underestimated the planet's age.

LIFE ON EARTH

A span of billions of years is difficult to imagine. Here's one way to picture that great expanse of time:

Picture the history of life on Earth as the length of a football field—100 yards (90 m). Life begins at one end of the field, about 3.5 billion years ago. The goal line at the other end of the field represents the present. Each inch (2.5 cm) represents about one million years. We start from the end of the field where life begins. As we cross midfield, life is still only single-celled creatures. Multicellular organisms don't appear until about 700 million years ago—only 20 yards (18 m) from the goal line. The first animals appear about 650 million years ago, 18 yards (16 m) from the present. The first vertebrates (animals having spinal columns) evolve 400 million years ago, on the 11-yard (10-m) line. The first mammals appear 225 million years ago, just 6 yards (5 m) from the goal line. And our own species, *Homo sapiens,* evolves within the last 1 million years, less than 1 inch (less than 3 cm) from the goal line!

In the twentieth century, science developed a more accurate estimate of the age of our world by measuring the radioactive elements contained in rocks. Scientists now estimate that Earth is about 4.5 billion years old. The oldest-known fossils—simple bacteria found in rocks from Australia—date back about 3.5 billion years. So life has had billions of years to evolve from simple cells to the life-forms we know today.

CREATURES PRODUCE MORE OFFSPRING THAN CAN SURVIVE For Darwin this was the key to the mystery of evolution. Picture a single oak tree. It produces thousands of acorns each year, enough to grow an entire for-est. But most acorns are eaten by insects, squirrels, birds, or other animals. Others decay after being infected by bacteria or fungi. Most of the acorns that sprout die from lack of sunlight or from drought or disease. Only a tiny fraction of the acorns produced by a single tree grow to maturity and produce more acorns themselves. Otherwise, the world would soon be covered with oak trees.

The same is true of all creatures. A salmon lays several thousand eggs, most of which are eaten before reaching maturity. Oysters produce millions of eggs, but only a very few survive. Natural selection has a lot of different individuals to choose from.

OFFSPRING RESEMBLE THEIR PARENTS Traits are passed from one generation to the next. A male and a female horse will produce a foal—a baby horse. They will never give birth to a cow or a pig. The foal won't be an exact copy of either parent. But it will inherit all the character-istics of a horse.

Almost every living cell has two complete sets of threadlike structures called chromosomes, one from each parent. The instructions of heredity—the genes—are car-ried on the chromosomes. When a creature reproduces, the chromosomes divide. Each sperm or egg cell gets only one set of chromosomes. When sperm and egg unite, the resulting embryo has one set of chromosomes from each parent, a mix of genes from the mother and the father.

Amazingly, Darwin knew nothing of how heredity

A foal is not an exact copy of its parents but has all the characteristics of a horse and shares specific traits with its parents.

works. In the mid-1800s, how offspring came to resemble their parents was still a mystery. But Darwin did understand this: parents pass traits on to their offspring.

INDIVIDUALS IN A SPECIES VARY IN SMALL WAYS When he returned to England, Darwin sorted and examined thousands of specimens from his voyage. Each individual specimen was different. Over and over again, Darwin compared two slightly different specimens and tried to decide if they were from different species or if they were variations within the same species.

No two individuals are exactly alike. We can see that when we look around a classroom or walk through a shopping mall. Each person is different in many, many ways.

Some differences are easy to see. People vary in height, weight, eye color, skin color, and dozens of other outward characteristics. Not all of these variations are hereditary, of course. Height and weight, for example, have a lot to do with our diet as well as the size of our parents. But both are determined at least in part by heredity. Tall parents tend to have tall children.

What's more, the differences we see are only a very small part of the story. We vary in thousands of ways that can only be seen with sophisticated tests. People vary in their ability to absorb oxygen into their bloodstream or their ability to digest sugars. Some people have quicker reaction times than others. The list goes on and on. In fact, people are different down to slight variations in the chemical makeup of our genes.

Individuals of other species vary too. To us, one cricket may look exactly like another. But scientific tests can find endless variation among individual crickets as well. The same is true of any other species you can name. As with humans, some variations are the result of environmental conditions—temperature or the availability of food, for example. But much variation is hereditary. Those hereditary differences can be passed on to the next generation.

NATURE "SELECTS" THE MOST SUCCESSFUL TRAITS Every creature competes in a world of limited resources. Any trait that gives an individual a slight advantage improves the chances that it will survive long enough to reproduce. This advantage is known as fitness. The advantage might be one of size, speed, or coloration. It might be a more efficient digestive system, the ability to survive with less water, or any of a thousand other slight variations. For example, a plant that germinates more quickly or grows taller might have an advantage over other seedlings. Its leaves would gather more sunlight. As it grows, it might shade out other plants, making it harder for them to compete.

An individual that lives long enough to reproduce passes on its characteristics—including the ones that gave it an advantage—to the next generation. Over many generations, more individuals with the advantage survive and reproduce. These helpful variations spread through a population. They become adaptations—characteristics of body structure or behavior that improve a species' ability to survive in an environment.

The blue crab has many adaptations for life in the warm, shallow waters along the Atlantic coast, for example. It has a hard shell and powerful claws for defense. It can crack open clams and snails and cut a dead fish into bite-sized pieces. A blue crab can crawl rapidly. Its paddle-shaped back legs make it an effective swimmer. A pair of eyes on raised eyestalks survey the environment for prey and for danger. The brownish green color of its back blends in with the mud of tidal creeks, so it can bury itself and virtually disappear.

Each of these adaptations developed through the long, slow process of evolution. An adult blue crab produces one or two million eggs. Only a very few survive to adulthood. Those survivors have traits that make them successful—strong shells, good eyesight, and protective coloration. Without those traits, crabs don't last long in waters full of other creatures looking for a crab dinner.

A crab that can't see nearby predators or one that is brightly colored so predators can see it won't live long

The blue crab has developed many adaptations to grow and survive in coastal waters.

enough to mate. And the trait that resulted in its becoming a meal for a hungry fish dies with it.

So the environment chooses the fittest individuals. Individuals with traits that give them the best chance of survival are most likely to live long enough to reproduce. Darwin called this natural selection.

ARTIFICIAL AND NATURAL SELECTION

After his voyage, Darwin studied how farmers and breeders of dogs and pigeons choose traits they want to establish in their plants or animals. There are hundreds of varieties of dogs. They vary in shape, from long, thin greyhounds to bulky, muscular bull terriers. They range in size from Chihuahuas to Great Danes. Some have long

hair, while others are short-haired. They even vary in behavior. Terriers are often nervous and high-strung, while
golden retrievers are known for their calm and peaceful
nature.

Despite all this variation, each of the many breeds be-
longs to the same species, *Canis familiaris.* Over many
generations, dog breeders selected particular characteristics they wanted in their animals. Dachshunds are hunting dogs bred to enter the burrows of small animals.
Pointers and setters were bred to hunt birds. Miniature
poodles and Pekingese were bred as small house pets.

This is artificial selection. Human breeders choose
traits they want to emphasize—size, shape, color, or
speed, for example. They then breed the dogs with the
best examples of that trait with one another. In a few
dozen generations, breeders can create a new variety of

**Thousands of years of selective breeding have brought
about many very different dog breeds.**

dog. In the well-documented history of dog breeding, this has happened hundreds of times.

Agriculture depends on artificial selection. Early humans harvested wild plants and domesticated wild animals. They selected plants or animals with the characteristics they most prized. They then planted the seeds or bred the animals with those traits. Farmers and agricultural companies still breed hardier, more productive varieties of vegetables, grains, and livestock every year.

Darwin realized that over time, nature also selects the best varieties. The challenges in a species' environment—predators, food scarcity, and climate, for example—choose individuals with traits that help them survive.

The English peppered moth is one well-known example. Years ago, most peppered moths were light gray. They were camouflaged to hide from birds on light gray tree bark. Then soot and ash from Britain's factories turned the trees darker. Lighter-colored moths became more likely to be eaten. Darker peppered moths, camouflaged to hide on the darker trees, were better able to survive. Most peppered moths were soon dark in color. In recent years, with less air pollution discoloring the trees, more light-colored moths are being found again. In each case, environmental conditions selected one variety of moth over another.

ADAPTATION IN ACTION

Here's one example of how the process works. Birds don't like the taste of monarch butterflies. A bird that eats one monarch rarely eats another. Now consider a tasty species of butterfly that looks a bit like a monarch. In each generation, some look more like monarchs than others. The better mimics are less likely to be eaten. They are more likely to survive and lay eggs. From that next generation, individuals that look most like a monarch will again be most likely to survive and breed. Over many generations, all the individuals in this species come to look very much like the bad-tasting monarchs.

Mimicry is an adaptation. Single individuals do not adapt to their environment. Individuals either survive to reproduce or they do not. Populations of organisms adapt, over many generations, through the process of natural selection. This is a very important idea, one that is often misunderstood. *Populations adapt and evolve. Individuals do not.*

The monach butterfly *(left)* and the viceroy *(right)* are nearly indistinguishable in appearance. The viceroy adapted over time to look like the bad-tasting monarch.

Biologists find examples of adaptation wherever they look. A flounder's mottled brown skin blends perfectly with the sandy bottom. When a small fish swims by, the flounder snaps it up before the unsuspecting meal even knows it's in danger. The flounder's camouflage is an adaptation. So is the coloration of toxic poison arrow frogs of the tropical rain forest. Their bright colors warn potential predators to stay away unless they want to swallow their last meal.

The idea of adaptation was a great contribution to biology. Before Darwin, biology simply described and catalogued the diversity of life. Now biologists can analyze any body structure or behavior they observe and can ask "Why did it evolve? What purpose does it serve?" As the evolutionary biologist Theodosius Dobzhansky said, "Nothing in biology makes sense except in the light of evolution."

People often compare Darwin's theory to another revolutionary idea—Nicolaus Copernicus's theory that Earth revolves around the Sun. Before Copernicus, people thought Earth was the center of the universe. Copernicus gave us a more realistic understanding of our own place in the cosmos. Earth turned out to be just a small planet circling an ordinary star somewhere in an endless ocean of stars.

Darwin's idea has had a similar effect. Before Darwin, many people viewed humans as the most important beings on our planet. Darwin's ideas allowed us to see ourselves more realistically. We are but one of the millions of species living on Earth. The rest of life did not evolve on Earth to serve our needs as the planet's dominant species.

CHAPTER 4

OBJECTIONS AND ADDITIONS TO DARWIN'S THEORY

Darwin knew some people would see his work as an attack against the biblical story of creation. And his book did create controversy. Arguments against Darwin's theory began almost immediately after *The Origin of Species* was published. Sir Richard Owen, one of England's most noted naturalists, led the opposition. Joseph Hooker and Thomas Huxley, Darwin's friends and fellow scientists, defended his theory. Huxley took such an active role that he earned the nickname "Darwin's Bulldog." Darwin stayed out of the storm. He continued his work at Down House and left the defense of his ideas to others.

Most scientists soon accepted the idea of evolution. But they were less willing to accept natural selection, for two main reasons: First, there didn't seem to be enough time in Earth's history to allow natural selection to work. And second, the theory didn't explain how traits were passed from generation to generation.

THE TIME PROBLEM

Evolution through natural selection takes a long, long time—enough for millions of generations. In the mid-1800s, it seemed that Earth was just not old enough to support Darwin's idea. Geologists estimated it would take millions of years to produce the sedimentary rock they found on Earth's crust. That's a long time by human standards, but not nearly long enough for all of Earth's creatures to evolve.

William Thomson, Lord Kelvin, was the most respected physicist of the late 1800s. He calculated how long Earth

This cartoon portraying Charles Darwin as a monkey mocked the naturalist for his theory that humans are related to primates.

would have taken to cool from a ball of molten rock. His estimate was about twenty million years. Again, it wasn't enough time for the great diversity of life to evolve.

The time problem was resolved in the late 1890s, when scientists discovered radioactivity. Earth is warmed by radioactive energy deep inside the planet, so it cooled much more slowly than Kelvin estimated. As our understanding of radioactivity, geology, and the origins of the solar system grew, so did estimates of the planet's age. The current estimate—about 4.5 billion years—allows plenty of time for evolution by natural selection.

THE PROBLEM OF HEREDITY

No one in Darwin's day knew how heredity worked. Most naturalists thought traits of both parents mixed together in their offspring. But blending traits contradicts natural selection. If traits blend, differences disappear—much like what happens when you mix black and white paint. The original colors disappear in a shade of gray. If traits blended, individuals in a population would become more and more alike.

But Darwin's theory of evolution depends on variation.

Gregor Mendel

Each individual is slightly different, and those differences are most important. Individuals with the most useful differences survive and reproduce. Some scientists were unwilling to accept Darwin's theory without a clear explanation of heredity.

In 1865 an Austrian monk and biology teacher named Gregor Mendel discovered how traits are passed from generation to generation. Mendel exper-

COEVOLUTION

No species lives in isolation. Each creature is surrounded by many others. Some serve as food. Others provide shelter. Still others are predators or parasites. Other species are part of the environment to which each species must adapt.

Over time, creatures adapt to coexist with other species. This process is called coevolution. In many cases, coevolution is an arms race. Cheetahs, for example, have evolved stalking skills and tremendous speed to catch antelopes. Antelopes have evolved delicate senses to detect hunting cheetahs and the speed and agility to escape. Generation after generation, the fastest, stealthiest cheetahs and the quickest, most alert antelopes survive to reproduce.

Sometimes coevolution produces cooperation. For example, many kinds of ants have evolved farming relationships with aphids. Aphids are small, defenseless insects that suck the sap from tender plant shoots. The ants shepherd the aphids, carrying them from plant to plant and protecting them from predators. In return, the aphids produce a sweet, sticky substance that the ants use for food.

imented for years, breeding varieties of peas. He studied how certain characteristics—such as seed color and plant height—were passed from generation to generation.

After years of research, he realized that each parent plant passes specific traits to its offspring. Scientists later called the carriers of these traits genes. He found that traits don't blend. They are either passed on completely or not passed on at all. Even if a trait is a recessive trait and doesn't appear as a characteristic of an individual, it can still be passed on in the genes.

Darwin and his fellow scientists never heard of this discovery. Mendel's experiments were overlooked until 1900, sixteen years after his death. And it wasn't until the middle of the twentieth century that the new science of genetics showed us how heredity works. Genetic science has now established Darwin's theory as the foundation of modern biology.

Sexual Selection: Evolution and Gene Mixing

Late in his career, Darwin recognized another factor that helps drive evolution: sexual selection. Darwin wrote about sexual selection in a later book, *The Descent of Man* (1871). Other biologists, including Wallace, were doubtful at first. But the idea of sexual selection has since become an important part of the theory of evolution.

Many creatures reproduce asexually (without sex). Some, like bacteria or amoebas, simply divide or form buds that become new individuals. Other species produce only females. Each generation of females produces fertile eggs that develop into the next generation.

Why don't all species reproduce this way? Sex uses energy and resources that could be used for feeding, growing, and producing offspring. In plants, forming flowers and fruit takes energy that could otherwise make food-producing leaves. Sexual reproduction also requires males, and they produce no offspring at all. Why should half the population compete for food and burn energy

A female peacock selects her mate based on the quality of his tail, considering its size and the distribution of eye spots.

competing for females but produce no babies?

The big advantage of sexual reproduction is gene mixing. Asexual reproduction passes the same set of genes from one generation to the next. Each offspring is a clone, or genetic copy, of its parent. But sex encourages variation. Each time two members of a species mate, their genes are mixed. Offspring that get the most useful mix of genes are most likely to survive and reproduce. But other genes are passed on too. If a new environmental condition threatens the species, some individuals may carry genes for traits that can help them survive.

Females are often very choosy about which male to take as a partner. For example, peahens mate with peacocks with the best array of tail feathers. Other female birds choose a male with the most elaborate song. Female mountain goats, elephant seals, and gorillas choose a mate who can defeat his rivals in combat.

A male's display tells a female how good his genes are. A male with bright, colorful feathers, huge antlers, or a complex song has probably resisted diseases and parasites. If a female chooses him as a mate, her offspring may receive those traits too. Of course, a female peahen doesn't think to herself, "Hey, nice genes!" Her own genes program her to seek out certain characteristics by instinct.

PREADAPTATION AND VESTIGIAL ORGANS

Body structures don't always make sense. Sometimes it seems they could have been better "designed." Many creatures have vestigial organs, for example. These body parts no longer serve a purpose. Vestigial organs are leftovers from a species' evolutionary history.

Every human has an appendix—a small extension of the intestine that seems to have no function. Millions of years ago, human ancestors used the appendix to help digest fibrous plants. It is a vestigial organ—a remnant of earlier evolution. We no longer need an appendix, but we still have one. Similarly, snakes and whales still have pelvic bones, even though they no longer have hips or legs.

An organ that serves one purpose may later evolve to fill another. This process is known as preadaptation. A creature adapts by using an organ that already exists for some other purpose. Feathers, for example, may have once served for mating display or as insulation to keep dinosaurs warm. Only after millions of years did they evolve to become useful in gliding, and later flying, in their descendants, the birds.

Penguins *(left)* and flying fish *(right)* both evolved wings, but for different reasons.

Evolution can only work with traits a species already has. A bird will not suddenly develop gills. And a fish cannot suddenly sprout wings. However, a fish might gradually evolve larger fins that eventually allow it to soar above the waves. And over many generations, a kind of bird might develop webbed feet and a streamlined shape that lets it swim underwater. Because of these adaptations, our world is populated with flying fish and penguins. Neither animal developed its peculiar adaptations suddenly from scratch. The penguin's feet and wings and the flying fish's fins were preadapted and later evolved into a different use.

CHAPTER 5

EVOLUTIONARY THEORY AFTER DARWIN

The modern view of evolution combines Darwin's ideas with the science of genetics. This current theory is called the Modern Synthesis. (Synthesis is the combination of two or more ideas.) It is also known as neo-Darwinism. (*Neo* means "new.") The scientists best known for developing this view are J. B. S. Haldane and Theodosius Dobzhansky.

Haldane, a British biochemist, used mathematics to analyze the process of evolution. In the 1920s and early 1930s, he showed how Mendel's rules of heredity could produce evolution in populations of organisms.

Dobzhansky, a Ukrainian biologist who moved to the United States in 1927, studied fruit flies. He found that this species—and others—carry genes for a range of different variations. As environmental conditions change, a particular variant may become more or less common. In 1937 Dobzhansky published *Genetics and the Origin of Species.* His book explained evolution using what was known about genetics and heredity.

Many other scientists, including Ernst Mayr, George Ledyard Stebbins, and George G. Simpson contributed to the modern view of evolution. These scientists applied Mendel's rules of heredity to the evolution of the plants and animals they studied. By the middle of the twentieth century, scientists knew natural selection promotes genetic changes within a population of creatures.

Scientists learned that chromosomes contain a chemical called DNA (deoxyribonucleic acid). Each DNA molecule is a chain of hundreds of thousands of atoms. In 1953 a team of scientists led by James Watson and Francis Crick figured out the structure of the DNA molecule. Their discovery explained how hereditary information is passed on when organisms reproduce. A DNA molecule contains two distinct strands that together are shaped like a tiny spiraling ladder. It records genetic information in a series of thousands of pairs of bases—smaller molecules that form the rungs of the ladder. The four bases are adenine, cytosine, guanine, and thymine, known as A, C, G, and T for short. The order in which they are arranged forms a genetic code that contains all the instructions for a new organism. When a cell divides, the strands of DNA divide and make copies of themselves.

Genetics provides powerful new evidence for evolution. All living creatures, from the simplest algae to the most complex animals, share the same DNA language. Of course, each species' DNA is different. The DNA in trout embryos tells them to become trout, instead of dandelions or manatees. But the code itself is the same for all creatures. The three-base sequence G-A-T always means aspartic acid, one of the amino acids that are the building blocks of proteins. This is true no matter which organism DNA comes from.

This means all living things probably share a common ancestor. Every living creature is descended from an unbroken line of organisms that succeeded in the struggle for survival. That is an awe-inspiring idea. Every pine tree, every crab, every human being is alive because its parents reproduced successfully. And of course, its parents were alive because their parents reproduced successfully. That line of inheritance extends back to the beginning of life itself. All life on Earth is related. The evidence is in our DNA.

At the genetic level, evolution happens in two different ways. First, each species has wide variations within its gene pool—the collection of genes shared by an entire population. These variants are called alleles. For example, the differences in human eye color are the result of different alleles. As the environment favors one allele over others, the trait associated with it becomes more common. It may eventually become a characteristic of an entire species.

Second, genes can mutate, or change. When DNA divides, errors sometimes happen in the copying process. This produces a mutation. If a gene is copied incorrectly in a reproductive cell, the error may be passed to the next generation.

Genes also mutate when an outside factor such as a virus, radiation, or a chemical damages an organism's DNA. A virus, for example, may replace a piece of a cell's DNA with some of its own.

Many mutations are harmful. Organisms that carry them don't survive. But once in a great while, a mutation makes an individual more successful in the competition

The Belgian Blue, a rare breed of cattle, has a genetic mutation that increases muscle growth, so the cattle have bulging muscles and hardly any fat.

of life. When that happens, the mutation is passed on to offspring and becomes a part of the gene pool.

IS EVOLUTION SMOOTH OR BUMPY?

One of the biggest questions facing biologists in the twentieth century was: Does evolution occur in leaps, or is it a more gradual process?

Evolution that occurs in rapid spurts is called saltation, from the Latin word for "jump." In the early twentieth century, scientists who thought evolution occurred mainly through mutations and rapid jumps were called mutationists. Fossils seem to support their viewpoint. In sedimentary rocks, different species of fossils appear suddenly from one layer to the next with no intermediate steps. This suggests evolution may happen in bursts of rapid change.

Jumps could be caused by events that force a population to adapt rapidly to changing conditions. Saltation might also result from mutations. Mutations that produce a useful change would spread quickly through a population. Geneticist Richard Goldschmidt called individuals with such mutations "hopeful monsters."

However, jumps in evolution may not really exist. The fossil record is very incomplete. Most organisms die without leaving a trace. Perhaps intermediate fossils—sometimes called missing links—have simply not been found.

Biologists who favored the idea of slow, gradual change were called biometricians. They thought evolution resulted from a long series of slight variations. Even a complex organ such as an eye, biometricians said, could evolve gradually. A worm born with a slightly more sensitive eyespot, for example, would have a small advantage. It would be more likely to find food and avoid predators. A species' vision could evolve gradually as nature selected tiny improvements in each generation. Over millions of years, a few light-sensitive cells could evolve to become a true eye.

Toward the end of the twentieth century, biologists again argued about the pace of evolution. Stephen Jay Gould, the best-known evolutionary biologist of his time, thought evolution occurs as punctuated equilibrium. Species remain little changed for long periods, he said. This equilibrium, or steady condition, is interrupted by brief periods when populations quickly evolve into new species.

Richard Dawkins and Daniel Dennett led the argument that evolution takes place little by little through slight variations in the genes. In general, their view that evolution takes a slow, gradual path has won the day. However, biologists still recognize that, in rare instances, a useful mutation might give rise to a new species in only a few generations.

Chapter 6

The Tree of Life

Speciation

A species is usually defined as a group of creatures that can reproduce only among themselves. For example, breeds of dog vary widely in size, shape, and color, but they can still mate and produce puppies. They all belong to the same species. A fox looks much like a dog, but a fox and a dog cannot produce offspring. They are different species.

How do new species come to be? Biologists call the process speciation. The most important cause is isolation. A population of creatures becomes separated from the rest of its species by changes in geography or climate, migration, or even changes in behavior.

Any group has many variations within its gene pool. A small population of creatures probably won't have all the variations within its species. Its gene pool is limited to whatever variations happen to be present when it becomes isolated. This chance selection is called genetic drift. When that small group is isolated, it can no longer interbreed with the others. Over many generations, the characteristics of the separate populations drift apart as they adapt to different environments.

Imagine a population of fish isolated in a lake when a landslide cuts it off from a nearby river. The lake-dwelling fish might evolve rounded bodies adapted to still water. Their river-dwelling relatives need sleek shapes better suited to swift currents. Eventually, the two groups are so different that they can no longer interbreed, even if their separation ends. They have become two different species.

In Earth's history, the main process separating populations has probably been continental drift. This is the slow movement of sections of Earth's crust. Continental drift gradually changes the shape and location of the continents. Over millions of years, these movements separate or join landmasses and cause great climate changes.

Adaptive Radiation

When a small population of creatures settles in an isolated location, new opportunities for evolution arise. Each environment has many niches—particular ways organisms can take advantage of the resources in their habitat. Newcomers evolve to take advantage of various niches through a process called adaptive radiation.

The finches Darwin found living on the Galápagos Islands provide an excellent example of adaptive radiation. Biologists believe a small group of finches must have flown to these lonely islands from South America. Once they reached the islands, the birds evolved into a variety of different species.

Some Galápagos finches evolved heavy beaks to crack large seeds. Others have smaller beaks useful for eating smaller seeds. Still others evolved long, thin beaks for catching and eating insects. One species even uses its sharp beak to puncture the skin of seabirds and drink their blood. From a common ancestor, each species evolved to fill a different niche on the islands.

Roots and Branches

Both Darwin and Wallace imagined evolution as a branching tree. The tree of life represents the history of Earth's species. In greatest detail, the tree would show all

These sketches show four different types of finches that Charles Darwin found on the Galápagos Islands. Each bird was specially adapted for the environment of the island on which it lived.

creatures that have ever lived. Over time, groups of organisms branch off from one another. Most branches stop at dead ends. When none of the individuals in a species produce offspring, that species becomes extinct. Entire groups of creatures become extinct when all the species in that group fail to reproduce.

The tree of life is a useful image. It illustrates that all life is related. All creatures share the same roots in the earliest living things. The tree shows how each species is descended from its ancestors and how they are related.

However, the image of a tree can give a false impression. Life does not reach upward like a tree, progressing toward a higher goal. The highest branches simply represent life at the present time. They are not necessarily more advanced than earlier species.

At any moment, it's impossible to know which variations in a population may eventually evolve into a new species. When it first appears in an individual, a variation is only one of many traits. We can only know a new species has evolved after many generations, when that trait has become a characteristic of an entire population.

Facing page: **The tree of life can be depicted in many ways. The diagram at the top shows some of the branches of the three main living groups, called domains. The larger tree shows how some of the plants and animals of the Eukaryotes domain are related.**

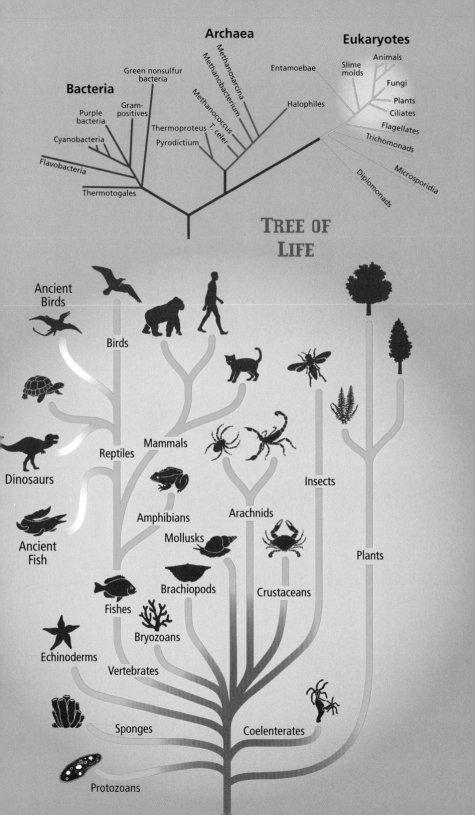

TREE OF LIFE

Bacteria

Flavobacteria

Cyanobacteria

Purple bacteria

Gram-positives

Green nonsulfur bacteria

Thermotogales

Pyrodictium

Thermoproteus

Archaea

Methanococcus

T. celer

Methanobacterium

Methanosarcina

Halophiles

Entamoebae

Eukaryotes

Slime molds

Animals

Fungi

Plants

Ciliates

Flagellates

Trichomonads

Microsporidia

Diplomonads

Ancient Birds

Birds

Reptiles

Dinosaurs

Ancient Fish

Mammals

Amphibians

Fishes

Echinoderms

Vertebrates

Sponges

Mollusks

Brachiopods

Bryozoans

Arachnids

Crustaceans

Insects

Plants

Coelenterates

Protozoans

As Darwin himself wrote, if we could somehow see all the creatures that ever lived, we couldn't tell where one species ended and another began. "[A]ll would blend together by steps as fine as those between the finest existing varieties."

THE LINNAEAN SYSTEM OF CLASSIFICATION

Scientists classify individual species into a series of broader categories. The method, devised by Swedish biologist Carolus Linnaeus, is often called the Linnaean system. You can think of it as a series of boxes within boxes. The smallest category is the species—a single kind of creature. Each species is grouped with other closely related organisms into a genus. In turn, each genus is grouped with similar genera (plural of genus) in a family and so on.

Here, for example, is the complete classification of the house cat:

Domain: Eucarida—organisms with a distinct cell nucleus
Kingdom: Animalia—animals
Phylum: Chordata—animals with nerve chords that pass along their back
Subphylum: Vertebrata—animals with backbones
Class: Mammalia—vertebrates that have hair, bear their young alive, and feed them milk
Order: Carnivora—mammals that hunt and eat meat
Family: Felidae—the cat family
Genus: *Felis*—small cats
Species: *catus*—the domestic cat

These categories tell us how the house cat is related to other creatures in the tree of life.

When biologists discovered the duck-billed platypus, they weren't sure at first how to categorize it.

THE PUZZLE OF CLASSIFYING ORGANISMS

Biologists sort species into larger groups, based on their similarities to other organisms. But classifying organisms can be tricky. Consider the puzzling case of the platypus. When specimens of this strange Australian animal first arrived in Europe, biologists thought someone was playing a joke. Here was an animal that swam in the water, had a snout like a duck's bill, and reproduced by laying eggs. It had fur like a mammal and venomous spines. Because the platypus feeds its young milk and is covered with hair, naturalists eventually agreed it should be included among the mammals.

Modern science gives biologists a powerful new tool to solve such problems. Scientists can now read the genetic code—the specific series of bases in any creature's DNA. They can also decipher the structure of proteins that DNA encodes. The more similar the proteins and DNA are, the more closely two species are related.

CHAPTER 7

THE HISTORY OF LIFE

MYSTERIOUS BEGINNINGS

Four billion years ago, Earth was a lifeless ball of rock. How did life on our planet first arise? Darwin didn't have an answer. However, in a letter to Joseph Hooker, Darwin imagined the first living creatures developed "in some warm little pond with all sorts of ammonia and phosphoric salts—light, heat, electricity present." Biologists still don't know how life began. But they can speculate.

Life almost certainly arose in the ocean. For many millions of years, rain poured down on the barren rock, dissolving minerals and washing them to the sea. Nitrogen, ammonia, carbon dioxide, and other gases in the early atmosphere dissolved in the rainwater. Meteorites crashed into Earth, contributing other important chemicals.

Could this chemical soup come to life, as Darwin guessed? In 1953 chemists Stanley L. Miller and Harold Urey conducted a famous experiment to test the possibility.

They dissolved the chemicals believed to exist in the early oceans in flasks of water. They added ammonia and methane, gases from Earth's early atmosphere. They passed electricity through the flasks to simulate lightning. And they shone powerful ultraviolet light on them, simulating the early Sun. They did not create life. But after several days, amino acids—the building blocks of proteins—had formed in the flasks. So the ingredients for life were present in the ancient oceans.

Somehow, after millions of years on lifeless Earth, molecules formed that could duplicate themselves. These molecules may have formed on the surface of rocks in tidal pools. They may have formed around the vents of undersea volcanoes or on clay sediments. They were not yet alive, but—like DNA—they could gather the chemicals needed to make copies of themselves.

SELF-CONTAINED PACKETS OF LIFE

The next big step in the evolution of life was the development of living cells. No one knows how the first cells formed. Somehow the replicating chemicals developed a protective cell membrane. Perhaps the first cells formed in bubbles of foam along the shore. Or maybe they formed when the molecules were trapped inside droplets of oil.

Cell membranes gave the replicating chemicals a great advantage: a cell can absorb chemicals through its membrane and not have to share them. As they grew, the cells reproduced by dividing. Eventually the seas were teeming with the first microbes—tiny single-celled organisms.

However it began, all life is probably descended from just one or a very few original life-forms. Why? Because all living things share the same DNA code.

The earliest evidence of life comes from ancient rocks in Greenland. These rocks contain tiny carbon deposits that are almost certainly the remains of living organisms. Radioactive dating places the rocks' age at about 3.85 billion years.

Many scientists think the first creatures were probably archaea. The name means "ancient ones." Although they look like bacteria, their DNA is very different. Modern archaea survive where other creatures would be cooked or frozen. Today, archaea populate the ocean and ocean sediments. They live in hot springs and undersea volcanic vents where the water temperature is more than 212°F (100°C.)

Once archaea arose, they must have spread quickly, gobbling up the chemicals they needed. As resources grew scarce, survival became a challenge. Each creature had to compete for the material it needed to grow and reproduce. From the earliest times, natural selection pushed life to evolve. Any variation that gave a creature an advantage was rewarded with more food and more opportunity to multiply.

PHOTOSYNTHESIS

Sometime early in the history of life, single-celled organisms began making sugars from carbon dioxide and water. This reaction, called photosynthesis, is powered by sunlight. Photosynthesis gave organisms a steady and reliable source of food.

Thick mats of algae grow along the shores of a pond.

Cyanobacteria—also called blue-green algae—evolved to gather energy from sunlight and produced their own food. These microbes formed dense mats in shallow waters. Similar mats of algae grow in ponds today. The oldest fossils—called stromatolites—are the ancient remains of these colonies. They are about 3.5 billion years old.

The early atmosphere was a mixture of nitrogen, carbon dioxide, methane, ammonia, and other gases. Modern creatures could never survive in such air. But photosynthesis releases oxygen. Over hundreds of millions of years, countless trillions of tiny organisms added oxygen to the air. Photosynthesis slowly changed Earth's atmosphere.

Oxygen was toxic to many early creatures. Many became extinct. Most of the survivors evolved to breathe oxygen, as we do today. Ozone—another form of oxygen—collected in the upper atmosphere. This ozone layer filtered out deadly ultraviolet light, which made the land more hospitable to life.

THE EUKARYOTE REVOLUTION

All the creatures mentioned so far are prokaryotes. Like modern bacteria and archaea, prokaryote cells have no nucleus. Their DNA is spread throughout the cell.

The next leap in evolution was the development of eukaryote cells. Eukaryote cells are much more complex than bacteria. Their DNA is enclosed in a nucleus. Eukaryote cells have other microscopic parts to carry out tasks such as energy production, movement, and food storage.

In 1970 biologist Lynn Margulis proposed a theory of how eukaryotes came into being. She noted that mitochondria and chloroplasts in modern cells both have their own DNA, separate from the DNA of the cell nucleus. This is evidence that they were once separate organisms—ancient bacteria.

Margulis imagined small microbes living inside larger ones. At first, these smaller microbes may have been predators or parasites. Gradually they developed partnerships with their hosts. Eventually, the cells grew dependent on one another. They became a single living organism. This partnership has conquered the world. All plants, all animals, all fungi, and all single-celled protozoa are eukaryotes.

How long ago did eukaryotes evolve? Researchers have found oil droplets that contain chemicals called sterols trapped in the rocks of northwestern Australia. Sterols help form cell membranes, and only eukaryote cells make them. The rocks are about 2.7 billion years old, so eukaryote cells have been around at least that long. But for 1.5 billion more years, all life on Earth remained single-celled and microscopic.

EXPLOSIONS OF LIFE

All multicellular creatures are eukaryotes. About 1.8 billion years ago, cells evolved cooperative behavior. They formed colonies and began to specialize. Some cells became muscle or specialized in digestion or in sensing the surrounding environment.

The earliest animals evolved in the oceans about 575 million years ago. They probably arose from colonies of single-celled creatures similar to today's sponges. About 530 million years ago, at the beginning of the Cambrian period, animal life of all sorts evolved to populate the ancient seas. Most of today's major animal groups evolved during this explosion of life-forms.

LIFE MOVES TO THE LAND

About 500 million years ago, plants were the first multicellular life to move to the land. They evolved stiff cell walls and the ability to move water from cell to cell. Plants also evolved spores—and later seeds—that could survive in dry conditions. Gradually plants spread across Earth, transforming the planet once again.

Invertebrates—animals without backbones, such as worms and insects—were the first animals to colonize the land, perhaps 450 million years ago. About 360 million years ago, vertebrates began moving to the land. Early amphibians evolved into reptiles. Eventually, from

DATING FOSSILS Fossils form when organisms die and their remains are buried in sediment. The layers of sediment build up, forming sedimentary rock. Minerals replace some of the molecules in the creature's body, turning it to stone. The fossil is preserved in the rock, like a leaf pressed between the pages of a book. The layers of rock provide one clue to a fossil's age. The deeper the layer, the older the rock must be.

Radioactive elements in the rocks and the fossils themselves also help scientists estimate their age. Every radioactive element has a certain half-life—the specific period of time in which half the original amount of that element decays into a different element. Measuring the radioactive elements and their decay products in a rock or fossil provides a good estimate of its age.

Carbon-14—a radioactive form of carbon—is used to date fairly recent fossils. Plants take in small amounts of C-14 in photosynthesis. Animals ingest the radioactive carbon when they eat plants or animals that have eaten plants. After it dies, an organism no longer takes in any carbon, of course. But the radioactive carbon continues to decay.

Scientists know how much C-14 is found in living organisms. So measuring the amount left in a fossil gives an estimate of how old it is. Carbon-14 has a half-life of 5,730 years, so it can only date fossils formed within the past 50,000 years. Beyond that age, not enough is left to measure. Scientists use longer-lasting radioactive elements to measure the age of fossils found in older rocks.

the deepest oceans to the tallest mountains, living creatures both large and small occupied every available habitat on Earth.

MAMMALS APPEAR

According to the fossil record, mammals evolved from reptiles about 225 million years ago. But dinosaurs dominated the world for many millions of years. Then came a great extinction at the end of the Cretaceous period, 65 million years ago. Mammals filled the many niches dinosaurs left behind when they died out. Warm-blooded mammals can stay active when temperatures are cool. They give birth to their young alive. And they feed their young with milk, enabling them to grow strong quickly. These advantages helped mammals spread across the planet.

HUMANS INHABIT THE GLOBE

Human beings have inhabited Earth for only a tiny fraction of its history. The first hominids (humanlike creatures) evolved from apes about 4.5 million years ago in Africa. Our own species, *Homo sapiens,* is less than 1 million years old. Perhaps highly developed brains helped them survive on the African plains without great speed or sharp teeth and claws. Like other apes, humans depended on social relationships. They lived in groups, protected one another, and helped each other gather food. Like other great apes, humans had opposable thumbs, useful for holding and grabbing. With the ability to walk upright, humans could use their hands to modify the environment with tools.

From Africa, humans migrated around the world. As they did, they changed the face of the planet. Humans hunted and fished, cleared the land to plant crops, and built structures for shelter. And as our species prospered, other species began to disappear.

This illustration depicts a meteorite striking Earth. Scientists think that such a catastrophe drove the dinosaurs to extinction.

MASS EXTINCTIONS

Extinction is an essential part of evolution. Over time, species disappear from Earth. "Species once lost do not reappear," Darwin reminds us. They are gone forever.

According to the fossil record, Earth has experienced a number of great extinctions. Sixty-five million years ago, something happened to wipe out the dinosaurs and many other species. Scientists searched for a cause of this great extinction for years. In 1980 Walter and Luis Alvarez announced that they had found traces of the element iridium in sediments from that time. Iridium is rare on Earth but common in meteors. The iridium they found probably came from an exploding meteorite, at least 6 miles (10 km) in diameter.

That collision must have thrown huge clouds of dust and smoke into the atmosphere, blocking sunlight and cooling Earth's climate. Many plants would have died. Without plants, such large animals as dinosaurs could not survive. More than two-thirds of Earth's species died out after that meteor strike. Recently scientists have found the meteor's likely point of impact—an undersea crater off the coast of Mexico's Yucatán Peninsula.

This event was not the worst mass extinction Earth has suffered, however. There is evidence for at least four others. The worst, at the end of the Permian period, killed about 90 percent of the species then living on Earth.

The causes for most of these catastrophes are still unknown. Climate changes, volcanic eruptions, meteor impacts, and continental drift may all have played a part. But there is no mystery about the extinction Earth is now experiencing. The cause is human activity. Agriculture, hunting, and the destruction of forests have extinguished thousands of species. Millions of years from now, future scientists, if they exist, may identify our time as another of Earth's great mass extinctions.

Chapter 8

The Misuse of Darwin's Ideas

Over the years, Darwin's ideas have been used to justify some very ugly human behavior. In the late 1800s, philosopher Herbert Spencer and others promoted social Darwinism. It considered the wealthiest, most successful members of society as the fittest of our species in the evolutionary sense. Social Darwinism gave people an excuse to use ruthless methods to rise to the top of the business and social world. It promoted the idea that the poor and downtrodden deserved their place in society. But it was a complete misreading of the concepts of evolution.

Evolutionary theory was also used to justify racism. In the late 1800s, Darwin's cousin Sir Francis Galton proposed that the human race could be improved by selective breeding. This idea was called eugenics. Eugenicists wanted only the strongest, smartest human beings to have children. In the first half of the twentieth century, eugenicists, including some in the United States, wanted to sterilize "inferior" groups of people. The movement reached its depths with

This field of genetically modified corn is resistant to the corn borer, an insect pest.

Adolf Hitler's program in the 1930s and 1940s to destroy Jews, Gypsies, and others he and his followers considered inferior to Germanic people.

In recent years, a few social scientists have tried to prove that some racial or ethnic groups perform more poorly on intelligence tests because of heredity. This, too, has been discredited. Differences among individuals within any group far outweigh any differences between entire groups of people.

GENETIC ENGINEERING

Scientists in the twenty-first century can transfer genes from one individual to another and even from one species to another. The process is called genetic engineering. This enables vats of bacteria to produce medicines or other useful products. Cows can be genetically engineered to produce medicines in their milk. Scientists use

This sheep named Dolly was the first cloned mammal.

genetic engineering to produce disease- and insect-resistant crops. We may even be able to cure diseases caused by defective genes. Scientists are also learning to clone individuals by transferring genetic material into an egg cell from which the nucleus has been removed.

But genetic engineering and cloning raise questions about eugenics once again. Is it right to tamper with the process of human reproduction? If we can make our children stronger or smarter through genetic engineering, should we? Is it wise to take control of evolution by inserting genes from one species into the DNA of another?

EVOLUTION ON TRIAL

After 150 years, *The Origin of Species* still stirs up controversy. Some people in the United States and elsewhere question the teaching of evolution in public schools. They believe it contradicts the lessons of the Bible. They've raised objections in state legislatures, school board meetings, and the courts.

The most famous court case was the Scopes trial in 1925. At that time, Tennessee law prohibited the teaching of evolution. A high school biology teacher, John Scopes, was convicted of teaching Darwin's theory and was fined one hundred dollars. The U.S. Supreme Court finally overturned that decision in 1968, in the case *Epperson v. Arkansas.* The Court ruled that laws banning the teaching of evolution violate the constitutional separation of church and state.

Since then some legislators and school boards have tried to require public schools to balance teaching evolution with the teaching of "creation science" or "intelligent design." But these explanations for the diversity of life are based on religious teachings. So far, efforts to include them in the public school curriculum have been derailed by courts or by public opinion.

Might the creatures we create damage the environment in unforeseen ways? Questions like these will become more urgent and more difficult to answer as our understanding of genetics and evolution increases.

GLOSSARY

adaptation: any feature that improves an organism's ability to survive in its environment

adaptive radiation: the process by which creatures colonizing a new habitat gradually evolve to fill various niches

allele: one variation of a specific gene

archaea: single-celled organisms similar in appearance to bacteria but very different in their genetic makeup

biometrician: an early evolutionary biologist who believed evolution proceeds gradually through small variations

chloroplast: the structure in plant cells that turns sunlight into energy

chromosome: the threadlike structure in a cell nucleus that contains DNA

clone: a genetic duplicate of an individual; to create such a duplicate

coevolution: the process by which two species affect each other's evolution

cyanobacteria: blue-green algae; single-celled organisms that carry out photosynthesis

DNA (deoxyribonucleic acid): a huge molecule found in living cells that carries an organism's genetic information

eukaryote: a complex cell that has a nucleus containing its DNA, as well as other structures that carry out the cell's functions

evolution: changes in the characteristics of a population over many generations

fitness: the ability of an individual to survive the challenges of its environment

fossil: the remains of an ancient creature found in a layer of sedimentary rock

gene: a section of DNA that is associated with a particular trait

gene pool: all the genes existing in a population at any time

genetic drift: random changes in the gene pool of a population

genetics: the science of heredity

homologous: similar in evolutionary origins, such as a bird's wing and a mammal's forelimb

mimicry: an adaptation in which one species evolves to look much like another

mitochondria: structures in eukaryote cells that turn food into energy

mutation: a change in DNA caused by a copying mistake, a virus, radiation, or a chemical reaction

natural selection: the process by which environmental factors choose certain variations within a population to become more common

nucleus: the central part of a eukaryote cell that contains the DNA

preadaptation: the process in which an organ originally used for one purpose later evolves to carry out a different function

prokaryote: a cell in which DNA is found throughout the organism, rather than in a nucleus. Bacteria and archaea are prokaryotes.

punctuated equilibrium: the theory that evolution occurs in rapid bursts interspersed with long periods of little change

recessive trait: a trait that is associated with alleles included in an organism's DNA but is not expressed in its growth and development

saltation: rapid evolutionary change, from the Latin word for "jump"

speciation: the process by which new species form

species: a single type of organism that is able to reproduce only with others of its own kind

survival of the fittest: the idea that those individuals best adapted to their environment are most likely to survive

variations: the slight differences between individuals within a species

TIMELINE

CA. **4.5 billion years ago**—Planet Earth formed.

CA. **4.4 billion years ago**—Oceans form as Earth cools.

CA. **3.85 billion years ago**—The first life on Earth appears.

CA. **3.5 billion years ago**—Stromatolites, the oldest-known fossils, form.

CA. **2.7 billion years ago**—The first eukaryotes, cells with nuclei, appear.

CA. **700 million years ago**—The first multi-cellular creatures exist.

CA. **650 million years ago**—Animals appear on Earth.

CA. **530 million years ago**—The Cambrian explosion occurs. Fossils of most groups of animals first appear.

CA. **450 million years ago**—Animals move to the land.

CA. **400 million years ago**—The first vertebrates appear.

CA. **225 million years ago**—The first mammals evolve from reptiles.

CA. **65 million years ago**—Dinosaurs become extinct.

CA. **4.5 million years ago**—The first humanlike creatures appear.

1 million years ago—The first *Homo sapiens* appear.

CA. **350 B.C.**—Greek philosopher Aristotle catalogs living specimens, dividing species into categories.

1658—Archbishop James Ussher calculates that God created the world on October 22, 4004 B.C.

1735—Carolus Linnaeus creates a system for classifying organisms.

1798—Thomas Malthus publishes *Essay on the Principle of Population.*

CA. **1809**—Jean-Baptise de Lamarck suggests that species evolve toward greater complexity.

1830—Charles Lyell publishes *Principles of Geology.*

1831—The *Beagle* sails with Charles Darwin as ship's naturalist.

1839—Darwin publishes his journal of the *Beagle*'s voyage.

1844—Darwin writes the first draft of *The Origin of Species.*

1858—Darwin receives a letter from Alfred Wallace describing his theory of evolution. Darwin's manuscript and Wallace's paper are read before the Linnaean Society on July 1.

1859—Darwin publishes *The Origin of Species by Means of Natural Selection.*

1866—Gregor Mendel publishes the basic principles of heredity.

1882—Darwin dies on April 19.

1900—Mendel's theory of heredity is rediscovered by biologists.

1925—John Scopes is convicted of teaching evolution in Tennessee public schools.

1937—Theodosius Dobzhansky publishes *Genetics and the Origin of Species.*

1953—James Watson and Francis Crick discover the structure of DNA.

1968—In *Epperson v. Arkansas,* the U.S. Supreme Court rules that laws prohibiting the teaching of evolution in public schools are unconstitutional.

1970—Lynn Margulis proposes the theory of how eukaryotes came into being.

1972—Niles Eldridge and Stephen Jay Gould publish a paper on the idea of evolution as punctuated equilibrium.

1976—Richard Dawkins publishes *The Selfish Gene.*

2000—Scientists decode the human genome—all the information in human DNA.

2005—The Kansas Board of Education discusses requiring that other theories of the beginning of life, such as intelligent design, be taught in public schools.

BIOGRAPHIES

GEORGES-LOUIS LECLERC DE BUFFON (1707–1788) The French naturalist Buffon is best known for dividing the history of the world into geological epochs. He was a founder of the science of paleontology (the study of fossils). Buffon's work suggested that Earth was much older than most people thought at the time. Buffon was the author of a huge study of natural history, *Histoire Naturelle.* It attempted to describe all that was known in biology, geology, and anthropology.

GEORGES CUVIER (1769–1832) Cuvier was one of the founders of paleontology. He served as professor of zoology at the Museum of Natural History in Paris, France. Cuvier examined and compared fossil animals. He was an expert at reconstructing the anatomy of the fossil creatures. His work established the existence of animals that are now extinct. He supported the idea that catastrophes such as the biblical flood had caused sudden, drastic changes to Earth.

CHARLES DARWIN (1809–1882) Charles Darwin was the son of a wealthy doctor and grandson of an early supporter of the idea that life on Earth evolves. As a young man, he served as a scientist on the *Beagle's* five-year voyage. Darwin's greatest work, *The Origin of Species by Means of Natural Selection* (1859), proposed that evolution comes about through a process of natural selection. Even without his theory of evolution, Darwin would have been a highly respected scientist. His studies of plant reproduction, earthworms, coral reefs, barnacles, carnivorous plants, and other creatures were admired for their detail and thoroughness. Darwin was ill for most of his adult life. He may have been infected with a parasite during his voyage to South America. He is buried in Westminster Abbey in London.

RICHARD DAWKINS (B. 1941) Dawkins is a British evolutionary biologist who promotes the idea that genes are the most important unit of evolution. According to Dawkins, genes evolve and replicate as the creatures that carry them experience evolutionary success. Dawkins, who was born in Kenya, serves as a professor at Oxford University in England. He has written a number of books for popular audiences, including *The Selfish Gene* and *Unweaving the Rainbow.*

THEODOSIUS DOBZHANSKY (1900–1975) Dobzhansky was a geneticist who was born and educated in Ukraine but moved to the United States in 1927. Dobzhansky's experiments with fruit flies showed that evolution takes place at the genetic level. He is credited with combining Darwin's theory of evolution with the science of genetics in his 1937 book *Genetics and the Origin of Species.* He also wrote a number of other books and more than four hundred research papers.

STEPHEN JAY GOULD (1941–2002) Gould was a paleontologist and evolutionary biologist. His best-known contribution to evolutionary theory was the idea of punctuated equilibrium. This idea, developed with Niles Eldredge, suggests that evolution occurs rapidly over relatively short periods of time. These rapid bursts of change are interspersed with long periods during which species change very little. Gould wrote essays and books on evolution for popular audiences. His clear, elegant writing made him one of the most widely read scientists of his time.

JOSEPH HOOKER (1817–1911) Botanist Joseph Hooker was a close friend of Charles Darwin. Along with Charles Lyell, Hooker arranged for the first reading of Darwin's and Wallace's papers on evolution in 1858. Hooker then became an active public supporter of Darwin's ideas. Hooker was the director of Britain's Royal Botanic Garden. He traveled widely in search of plant specimens and wrote books and articles describing his discoveries. Hooker's study of plant species and their distribution around the globe gave much support to Darwin's theory.

JAMES HUTTON (1726–1797) James Hutton was a Scottish farmer, doctor, and geologist. He first outlined evidence that Earth is extremely old and that its features form gradually over long periods of time. Hutton's ideas were revolutionary for his time. He claimed natural processes could explain the geology of Earth, without having to rely on biblical events such as the great flood.

THOMAS (T. H.) HUXLEY (1825–1895) After Darwin's controversial theory was published, T. H. Huxley was his most outspoken defender. Huxley supported the theory of evolution in meetings, speeches, and his many writings, while Darwin remained quietly in the background. These efforts won him the nickname "Darwin's Bulldog." Huxley was a respected naturalist and philosopher in his own right, known for his studies of invertebrate animals, fossils, and the evolution of vertebrates.

JEAN-BAPTISTE DE LAMARCK (1744–1829) French nobleman and naturalist Lamarck was an early proponent of the idea that life evolves. He believed fossil animals must be the ancestors of modern creatures. Lamarck spent much of his life studying plants, and later, invertebrate animals. He was the first to classify animals into vertebrates and invertebrates. Lamarck was also the first scientist to use the term *biology*. Lamarck believed that organisms evolve through the use or disuse of their organs.

CHARLES LYELL (1797–1875) Charles Lyell was a Scottish geologist and lawyer. Expanding upon James Hutton's work, Lyell's *Principles of Geology* described a world that changes gradually over vast periods of time. It displaced the earlier idea that the world's geological features were formed suddenly by great upheavals and catastrophes. In 1858 Lyell and Joseph Hooker arranged for the first public reading of Darwin's and Wallace's papers on the theory of evolution. Lyell did not agree with Darwin's ideas at first. He later accepted Darwin's theory, and his writings in the mid-1860s provided geological support for it.

LYNN MARGULIS (B. 1938) Lynn Margulis is a geneticist best known for her theory that eukaryotes arose from simpler cells. The strongest evidence for this is the fact that chloroplasts and mitochondria—organelles found in modern cells—have their own DNA, separate from the cell's DNA. She believes much of evolution takes place through interactions among species. She is the author of both scientific books and a number of popular works with her son, Dorian Sagan. Margulis received the Presidential Medal of Science in 1999.

GREGOR MENDEL (1822–1884) Gregor Mendel was the founder of the science of genetics. Mendel's experiments with peas revealed how specific traits are passed from one generation to the next. In 1866 Mendel reported his results in an article entitled "Experiments with Plant Hybrids." His findings were ignored by biologists until 1900. Sxteen years after his death, Mendel was finally credited with discovering the basic principles of heredity.

ALFRED RUSSEL WALLACE (1823–1913) Alfred Wallace was the codiscoverer of the theory of evolution. In 1848 Wallace began a four-year expedition to Brazil. In 1854 Wallace left England again on a seven-year expedition to the South Pacific. He supported his studies by collecting specimens. In 1858 he wrote a paper describing a theory of evolution very similar to Darwin's. As a result, Darwin was forced to announce his own theory earlier than he had planned. Wallace returned to England as a highly respected scientist. He led an amazingly productive life, completing twenty-one books and hundreds of scientific articles and essays.

SOURCE NOTES

15 Charles Darwin, *The Origin of Species by Means of Natural Selection* (New York: The Modern Library, 1936), 53.

20 Andrew Berry, ed., *Infinite Tropics: An Alfred Russel Wallace Anthology* (London: Verso, 2002), 56.

33 Daniel Dennet, *Darwin's Dangerous Idea* (New York: Simon and Schuster, 1995), 147.

52 Charles Darwin, *The Origin of Species,* rev. ed. (New York: W. W. Norton & Company, 2002), 98.

54 John van Wyhe, "Chapter IV. The Spread of Evolution," *The Writings of Charles Darwin on the Web,* May 10, 2005, http://pages.britishlibrary.net/charles.darwin/texts/letters/letters2_04.html (May 19, 2005).

62 Charles Darwin, *The Origin of Species by Means of Natural Selection*, 256.

SELECTED BIBLIOGRAPHY

Darwin, Charles. *The Origin of Species by Means of Natural Selection.* New York: The Modern Library, 1936.

———. *The Voyage of the Beagle.* New York: New American Library, 1972.

Dawkins, Richard. *The Blind Watchmaker: Why the Evidence of Evolution Reveals a Universe without Design.* New York: W. W. Norton and Company, Inc., 1986. Reprint, 1996.

———. *Unweaving the Rainbow.* Boston: Mariner Books, 2000.

Gould, Stephen Jay. *Bully for Brontosaurus.* New York: W. W. Norton and Company, Inc., 1991.

Larson, Edward J. *Evolution.* New York: The Modern Library, 2004.

Mayr, Ernst. *What Evolution Is.* New York: Basic Books, 2001.

Shermer, Michael. *In Darwin's Shadow.* New York: Oxford University Press, 2002.

Zimmer, Carl. *Evolution: The Triumph of an Idea.* New York: HarperCollins, 2001.

FURTHER READING

Graves, Renee. *The Scopes Trial.* New York: Children's Book Press, 2003.

Green, Gen. *Evolution.* Farmington Hills, MI: Blackbirch Press, 2004.

Jenkins, Steve. *Life on Earth: The Story of Evolution.* Boston: Houghton Mifflin, 2002.

Sloan, Christopher, et al. *The Human Story: Our Evolution from Prehistoric Ancestors to Today.* Washington, DC: National Geographic, 2004.

Sproule, Anna. *Charles Darwin: Visionary behind the Theory of Evolution.* Farmington Hills, MI: Blackbirch Press, 2002.

Stefoff, Rebecca. *Charles Darwin and the Evolution Revolution.* New York: Oxford University Press, 1998.

Thompson, Bruce, ed. *Evolution (Fact or Fiction).* Farmington Hills, MI: Greenhaven Press, 2003.

WEBSITES

About Darwin.com
http://www.aboutdarwin.com/
This is a website dedicated to Darwin's life and work.

The Alfred Russel Wallace Page
http://www.wku.edu/~smithch/index1.htm
This website presents detailed information on the codiscoverer of the theory of evolution.

Evolution
http://www.pbs.org/wgbh/evolution/
This website contains extensive information and resources. It is a supplement to the PBS series on evolution and Carl Zimmer's companion book.

Tree of Life Web Project
http://tolweb.org/tree/phylogeny.html
This website explores the diversity of life on Earth.

INDEX